REVOLUTIONIZING EDUCATION

Implementing NEP 2020 For Industry Ready Graduates

REVOLUTIONIZING EDUCATION

Implementing NEP 2020 For Industry Ready Graduates

Bhavesh Kumar Gadhethariya

Available on amazonkindle

Worldwide Published by

Pendown Press

PREMIUM BUSINESS PUBLISHER

PENDOWN PRESS LLP

An ISO 9001 & ISO 14001 Certified Co.,

Regd. Office: 3767A, Kanhaiya Nagar,

Tri Nagar, Delhi-110035

Ph.: 8130886000, 9650072927

E-mail: info@pendownpress.com

Branch Office: 1A/2A, 20, Hari Sadan, Ansari Road,

Daryaganj, New Delhi-110002

Ph.: 011-45794768

Website: PendownPress.com

Edition: 2025

Price: ₹ 399

ISBN: 978-93-6338-459-0

Layout and Cover Designed by Pendown Graphics Team

Printed and Bound in India by Thomson Press India Ltd.

Dedication

Dedicated to the educators who inspire change, to the learners who chase their dreams, and to all those working together to create a brighter future for generations to come.

Table of Contents

Acknowledgements

An Expression of Heartfelt Gratitude

I want to take a moment to express my heartfelt thanks for the opportunity to share my journey with you. This book is not just a collection of words; it's the result of years of hard work, learning, and personal growth. My hope is that the stories and insights within these pages will inspire and resonate with you in meaningful ways.

To My Family

First and foremost, I owe a deep debt of gratitude to my parents. Your unwavering strength and wisdom have been the guiding lights on my path, shaping who I am today and fueling my achievements.

To my incredible wife, Rina Gadhethariya, you are my rock and my greatest supporter. This journey would not have been possible without your endless love and patience. You are the heart of everything I do.

To my wonderful son, Anant Gadhethariya, your laughter and enthusiasm bring joy to my life and motivate me to reach new heights. You remind me daily of what truly matters.

Acknowledging My Mentors and Peers

I also want to extend my thanks to my mentors, colleagues, and the vibrant community of thinkers and doers around me. Your insights and support have been invaluable in my growth. I am deeply grateful for your encouragement and guidance throughout this journey.

A special shoutout goes to my friend Dinesh Verma, CEO of Pendown Press, along with his dedicated team. Your steadfast support and constructive feedback have made a significant impact on this creative process.

Celebrating Our Collective Journey

To everyone mentioned here and those whose names may not appear, your contributions have been essential to this journey. Together, we've created something truly special, and I look forward to continuing this adventure of growth and success with all of you.

Thank you for being part of this shared experience.

Preface

In a country as diverse and vibrant as India, education plays a crucial role in shaping the future. It is not merely a means to acquire knowledge but a pathway to empowerment and growth for individuals and society as a whole. Over the years, the Indian education system has undergone significant changes, influenced by historical developments, cultural shifts, and evolving societal needs. Yet, despite these efforts, challenges persist, and there is a growing recognition of the need for reform.

The National Education Policy (NEP) 2020 presents an opportunity for profound transformation. This policy aims to redefine education in India by emphasizing holistic development, innovative teaching methods, and the integration of technology. It aspires to create a more inclusive system that caters to the diverse needs of students and prepares them for the complexities of the modern world.

This book delves into various aspects of the Indian education landscape, examining the NEP 2020's vision and its potential impact on both school and higher education. From understanding the core principles behind the policy to exploring the practical challenges of implementation, each chapter provides insights into how we can work together to create a brighter future for our students.

As we navigate through the complexities of educational reform, it is essential to acknowledge the role of various stakeholders—educators, policymakers, parents, and the community. Together, we can foster a culture of lifelong learning and innovation, ensuring that the next generation is equipped with the skills and knowledge needed to thrive in a dynamic global environment.

In closing, I invite you to engage with this book as a call to action. Let us join hands in our quest for a transformative education system that empowers every learner and embraces the promise of a better tomorrow.

Let's start then!

Regards,

Bhavesh Kumar Gadhethariya

Know Your Author

With over two decades of entrepreneurial experience, Bhavesh Kumar Gadhethariya has been at the forefront of innovation in the education, IT, and travel industries. Since 2004, he has been leading the Infinity Group of Companies, playing a key role in the fields of education, travel, and information technology. Under his guidance, Infinity has grown steadily and earned a strong reputation for its forward-thinking approach. One of the major milestones includes PayTM investing in Infinity Transoft Solution Pvt. Ltd. as a strategic partner, supporting its future growth.

He holds a Bachelor's degree in Information Technology (2004) and an MBA in IT (2007), and is currently pursuing a Ph.D. in Artificial Intelligence (since 2022). Over the years, he has been deeply involved in designing and developing software — from understanding client needs, creating system plans, coding, testing, and fixing errors, to successfully delivering the final product.

Known for his clear communication and leadership, he has managed various projects by planning properly, using resources wisely, and making sure teams work smoothly. His interests include data analysis, artificial intelligence, and business intelligence, and he continues to explore new ways to bring smart, tech-driven solutions to everyday challenges.

In his entrepreneurial roles, he currently serves as:

- **Managing Director (since 2008)** of *Infinity Infoway Limited.*, Rajkot, Gujarat
- **Managing Director (since 2012)** of *Infinity Transoft Solution Pvt. Ltd.*, Rajkot, Gujarat (with Series A investment from PayTM)
- **Director (since 2021)** of *Infinity Edutech Pvt. Ltd.*, Rajkot

His work has been honored both in India and abroad. One of his most prestigious achievements is receiving the National Award for Outstanding Entrepreneurship in MSEs (Services), presented by Mr. Pranab Mukherjee, the then President of India. He has also received:

- The SKOCH Award (2019) for Educational Resource Planning
- Two Prawaas Awards (2017) – for Excellence in Innovation and Best Content Display
- Recognition at WES 2024 in Dubai, UAE, as Asia's Leading ERP Solution Provider

As someone closely connected with both the education field and digital technology, he saw that many people were confused about the National Education Policy (NEP) 2020. Although there is a lot of information available online, it is often scattered and difficult to understand. To solve this problem, he decided to bring all the important points together in one simple and clear book. This way, teachers, students, parents, and anyone interested in education can easily understand what the policy really means.

With this book, his aim is to make NEP 2020 easy to understand, start meaningful discussions, and help more people take part in the changes coming to Indian education. His goal is to share knowledge in a way that makes the policy not just easy to read, but also useful for everyone.

Chapter 1

Introduction to the Indian Education System

Overview of the Indian Education Landscape

India's education system is one of the largest in the world. It serves over 300 million children and is structured under a federal framework, where both central and state governments play significant roles in policy-making and implementation. The system encompasses several layers, including pre-primary, primary, secondary, and higher education, along with vocational and skill development institutes. From public schools to private institutions, India's education sector is multifaceted, addressing the needs of urban, semi-urban, and rural populations.

India's education system has made notable strides since independence in 1947, particularly with the introduction of the Right to Education Act in 2009, which guarantees free and compulsory education for children aged 6 to 14 years, ensuring that no child is left behind. Programs like Sarva Shiksha Abhiyan have also made education more accessible, aiming to bring every child into the fold of learning.

However, while progress has been made, the education system still faces challenges. There are differences in the quality of education between cities and villages, and many students in rural areas still struggle to get the same opportunities as those in urban schools. These gaps remind us of the work that remains to be done.

Historical Development of the Education System in India

India has a rich and diverse history of education that dates back thousands of years. In ancient times, education was imparted in **Gurukulas**, where students lived with their teachers (gurus) in close-knit, residential settings. These institutions emphasized holistic learning, covering subjects such as **philosophy, mathematics, astronomy, medicine, arts, and languages**. Education was not confined to rote memorization or examinations—it was about **understanding life, self-discipline, and developing character.**

Importantly, ancient Indian education was **practical and multi-disciplinary.** Learning often occurred through observation, discussion, and real-life application. For example, in the **Mahabharata**, the **Pandavas** each received specialized education based on their aptitude and role in society: **Arjuna** mastered archery, Bhima trained in physical strength and warfare, **Yudhishthira** in dharma and statecraft, **Nakula and Sahadeva** in medicine, animal husbandry, and swordsmanship. This showcases how education was tailored to individual strengths and integrated various disciplines—a principle now being re-emphasized in modern educational reforms.

With the arrival of the British in India, the education system underwent significant changes. The British introduced a more formal and standardized system, focusing on classroom instruction and examinations. English became the primary medium of instruction, and institutions such as the University of Calcutta, University of Bombay, and University of Madras were established in the 19th century. While this system expanded access to education, it also emphasized rote learning and marginalized India's indigenous knowledge systems.

After independence, India recognized the need to build an inclusive and equitable education system. The government established key institutions like the University Grants Commission (UGC) to oversee higher education and the All India Council for Technical Education (AICTE) to regulate technical programs.

The **first National Education Policy (NEP)** in 1968 introduced the 10+2+3 structure and aimed to promote a unified educational framework. However, it faced challenges such as poor implementation and insufficient funding. In 1986, a revised NEP emphasized universal access to education and the development of open universities. The 1992 revision of this policy placed additional focus on women's education, primary education, and adult literacy.

The most transformative step came with the launch of the National Education Policy 2020, which seeks to revive and modernize India's educational roots. NEP 2020 encourages multi-disciplinary learning, critical thinking, vocational training, and experiential learning—ideas that resonate with the Gurukula model of ancient India. It also promotes education in mother tongues, the integration of arts and sciences, and emphasizes individualized learning paths, much like how the Pandavas received tailored education suited to their abilities.

In essence, NEP 2020 marks a return to India's educational heritage—revitalizing ancient wisdom while aligning with global best practices—to prepare students not just for jobs, but for life.

Key Achievements and Shortcomings in Indian Education

Achievements:

- **Right to Education:** The Right to Education Act has been a game-changer. It ensures that every child, no matter where they come from, has the right to go to school and get an education. This has helped increase school enrollments, especially for girls and children from underprivileged backgrounds.
- **Growing Number of Schools and Colleges:** India has seen a significant rise in the number of schools, colleges, and universities. Institutions like the Indian Institutes of Technology (IITs) and Indian Institutes of Management (IIMs) are globally recognized for their excellence.
- **Government Initiatives:** Programs like the Mid-Day Meal Scheme have encouraged more children to attend school by providing them with nutritious meals, reducing dropout rates.
- **Technology in Education:** With the rise of digital learning platforms, students in even the most remote areas now have access to online classes and resources, making learning more flexible and accessible.

Shortcomings:

- **Quality of Education:** While many children are going to school, the quality of education in some areas remains poor. Teachers may be absent, schools may lack basic facilities, and students may not get the attention they need to thrive.

- **Urban-Rural Divide:** Children in cities often have better schools, more resources, and access to private coaching, while those in rural areas may struggle with limited resources, untrained teachers, and overcrowded classrooms.
- **Focus on Rote Learning:** In many schools, students are still encouraged to memorize information rather than understand it. This focus on rote learning can leave them unprepared for real-life challenges and problem-solving.
- **Dropout Rates:** Despite improvements, many children, especially from marginalized communities, drop out of school early due to financial pressures, lack of support, or poor learning environments.

Conclusion

India's education system has come a long way, but there's still a journey ahead. While we've made great strides in making education accessible to millions, challenges like quality, equality, and modern learning methods still need attention. Every child deserves a chance to learn and grow in a way that prepares them for a bright future. Together, with continuous efforts, we can build a system that nurtures every young mind and helps them achieve their dreams.

Chapter 2

Understanding NEP 2020: A Vision for the Future

What is NEP 2020?

The *National Education Policy (NEP)* 2020 is a groundbreaking framework introduced by the Government of India, aiming to revolutionize the country's education system. After almost 34 years since the last education policy, NEP 2020 was designed to bring much-needed changes that reflect the needs of the 21st century. Its goal is to create an education system that not only provides knowledge but also focuses on creativity, problem-solving, and skill development.

NEP 2020 is built on the foundational pillars of Access, Equity, Quality, Affordability and Accountability. Whether it's children in school or adults looking to enhance their skills, the policy opens doors for flexible and innovative learning opportunities. It emphasizes that education should be accessible and inclusive for all, bridging gaps between different social and economic groups. The policy aims to achieve significant reforms across all levels of education—from preschool to higher education—by 2030, making India a global knowledge superpower.

Core Principles and Objectives of NEP 2020

The policy aims to develop good individuals who are capable of rational thought and action, embodying compassion, empathy, courage, resilience, scientific temper, and creative imagination, all guided by ethical values.

It also focuses on building a sense of responsibility among citizens to contribute towards creating a society that is equal for all, inclusive of everyone, and accepted by all. The policy emphasizes building a strong educational system equipped with modern technology, a stimulating environment, and solid physical infrastructure.

The principles and objectives on which NEP 2020 is based are:

- **Recognizing, identifying, and fostering the unique abilities of every student**

  NEP 2020 emphasizes that every child is different and has unique strengths. The policy encourages both teachers and parents to work together to help students discover their interests and talents—be it in academics, sports, arts, or vocational skills. The aim is to develop each child holistically—mentally, emotionally, socially, and physically.

- **Ensuring foundational literacy and numeracy by Grade 3**

  The policy prioritizes the ability of all students to read, write, and perform basic mathematics by the end of Class 3. This foundational skill set is considered critical for future learning, and dedicated national missions and programs will support teachers and schools to meet this goal early in a child's education journey.

- **Providing flexibility in choosing programs and courses**

  Students will no longer be confined to rigid subject choices. They can choose subjects across streams—like science with music, or commerce with coding—according to their interests. This flexibility allows for a more customized and engaging learning experience.

- **Removing divisions between arts, science, curricular and extracurricular, and vocational and academic streams**

  NEP 2020 aims to break down the traditional boundaries between different disciplines. All subjects are given equal importance, allowing students to pursue a balanced education that includes academic knowledge, creative pursuits, physical activity, and vocational skills.

- **Promoting a multidisciplinary and holistic approach to education**

  Students will be encouraged to learn from multiple disciplines to understand the connections between subjects. For instance, a science student might also study history or design thinking. This approach prepares students for real-world challenges that are not confined to one field.

- **Placing emphasis on conceptual learning over rote memorization**

  Instead of encouraging students to simply memorize facts for exams, NEP 2020 focuses on understanding concepts deeply. Learning will be application-based, encouraging students to grasp the "why" and "how" behind every topic.

- **Encouraging creative and critical thinking**

  The policy promotes inquiry-based learning where students ask questions, explore ideas, and come up with innovative solutions.

It emphasizes the development of independent thinking, problem-solving, and decision-making abilities.

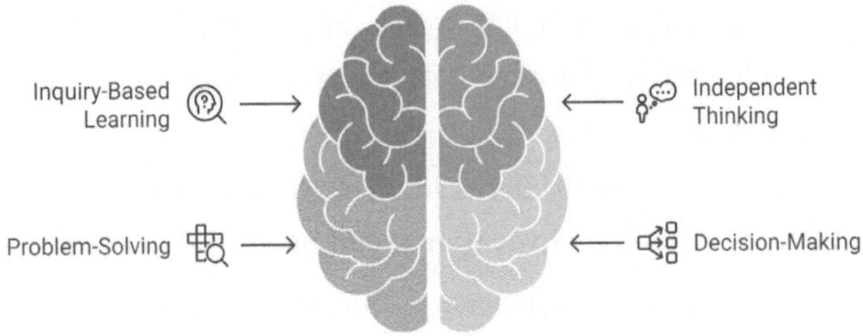

- **Enabling students to learn various languages**

  Multilingualism is encouraged, especially at the foundational level. Children will be taught in their mother tongue or regional language wherever possible until at least Grade 5. The policy also promotes the learning of classical and foreign languages, thereby strengthening communication skills and cultural awareness.

- **Equipping students with life skills**

  Along with academic content, students will be taught essential life skills such as communication, cooperation, teamwork, resilience, emotional intelligence, and adaptability—skills that are important in both personal and professional life.

Unveiling Essential Life Skills for Students

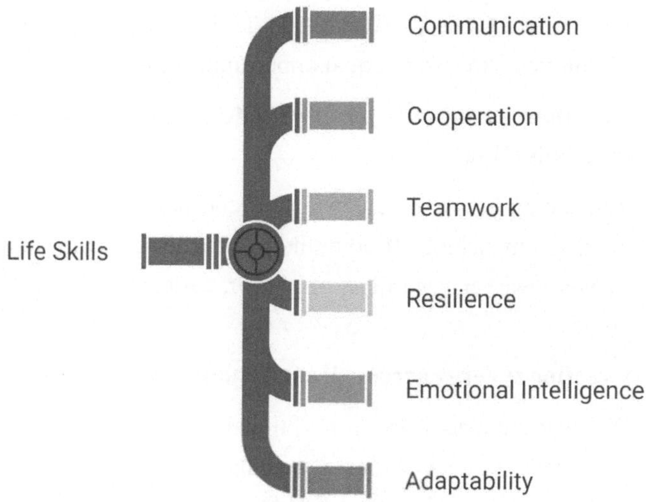

- **Advancing the use of technology in education**

  NEP 2020 supports the integration of technology in classrooms and administrative systems. From smart classrooms and digital learning tools to online courses and AI-driven teaching aids, technology will be used to make learning more effective and inclusive.

- **Ensuring respect for diversity and local contexts**

  The policy recognizes India's vast cultural, linguistic, and social diversity. Education will be tailored to local needs, customs, and languages, while still maintaining national standards. This ensures that students from all backgrounds feel represented and included.

- **Promoting equity among all students**

  NEP 2020 focuses on bridging the gap between different sections of society. Special support will be given to children from disadvantaged groups—such as girls, rural populations, Scheduled Castes, Scheduled Tribes, and children with disabilities—to ensure equal opportunities for all.

- **Including everyone in the education system without discrimination**

  The policy envisions an inclusive education system where no child is left behind. It commits to providing quality education to every learner, regardless of gender, caste, religion, income, or ability.

- **Creating synergy across all curriculums and learning systems**

  Whether students learn in traditional schools, online platforms, open schools, or vocational training centers, their experiences will be integrated into a unified framework. This synergy allows students to move seamlessly across different modes of learning and gain credit for all forms of knowledge.

- **Conducting regular reviews of student progress**

  The focus will shift from high-stakes board exams to regular, formative assessments that help track student development. These assessments will evaluate not just knowledge, but also skills, values, and attitudes, offering meaningful feedback to improve learning outcomes.

- **Encouraging ongoing research and innovation in education**

  Research will be promoted across all levels—from classroom practices to higher education innovations. Institutions will be supported to conduct research that can inform policy, improve pedagogy, and contribute to national development.

- **Recognizing education as a public service accessible to everyone**

  Education will be treated as a fundamental right and a public responsibility. Governments will be expected to ensure access to quality education for all, especially in underserved areas.

- **Supporting private sector participation for innovation and scale**

  The policy acknowledges the role of the private sector in enhancing access and quality. However, it calls for strong regulations to ensure that private institutions align with national goals and maintain transparency, accountability, and affordability. Partnerships will aim to blend innovation with equity.

Key Reforms Suggested in NEP 2020

NEP 2020 has brought forward some major reforms to reshape the education system. Here are some of the most significant changes:

- **School Structure Redefined:** The policy introduces a new curricular structure known as the **5+3+3+4 model**, which divides school education as:

Stage	Classes	Age Group
Foundational	Preschool – Class 2	3 – 8 years
Preparatory	Classes 3 – 5	8 – 11 years
Middle	Classes 6 – 8	11 – 14 years
Secondary	Classes 9 – 12	14 – 18 years

- **Mother Tongue as a Medium of Instruction:** Up to Grade 5, wherever possible, children will be taught in their mother tongue or regional language. This is to help young learners better grasp concepts and stay connected with their culture.

- **Higher Education Reforms:** The policy proposes that higher education institutions offer more flexibility, allowing students to choose their courses and even change streams. It also encourages multidisciplinary institutions and simplifies regulatory bodies to ensure that quality education is delivered across all fields.
- **Vocational Training from an Early Age:** Vocational education will now be introduced at the school level, so students can start learning practical skills early on. This will better prepare them for the job market.
- **Common Entrance Exams for Universities:** NEP 2020 suggests a common entrance exam for admissions to universities, reducing the burden of multiple exams and making the process more transparent.

Conclusion

In summary, NEP 2020 aims to create an education system that is fair and accessible to all, while helping students prepare for the future with new teaching methods and skill-building. It focuses on the overall growth of students, making sure they are ready to face challenges and succeed. With these changes, India hopes to build a strong education system that helps students become capable and positive contributors to society.

Chapter 3

How NEP 2020 Will Reform Indian Education

New Pedagogical and Curricular Structure: The 5+3+3+4 Model

One of the most significant changes introduced by NEP 2020 is the new educational structure known as the *5+3+3+4 model.* This framework divides a child's education into four stages:

➢ **Foundational Stage (5 years):** This includes three years of preschool (or Anganwadi) and two years of Grade 1 and 2. The focus is on developing basic literacy and numeracy skills through play and interactive learning.

- **Pedagogical Implications:** The pedagogy in this stage is rooted in early childhood care and education principles, emphasizing sensory development, curiosity, and emotional well-being. Learning happens through storytelling, songs, drawing, building blocks, and nature walks. Teachers act as facilitators, allowing children to learn through experiences rather than instruction.
- **Teaching Method:** Teaching at this stage is primarily play-based, involving storytelling, rhymes, hands-on activities, and learning through observation and daily life experiences. The

aim is to build curiosity, social skills, and basic understanding in a stress-free environment.

- **Preparatory Stage (3 years):** This covers Grades 3 to 5, where students are gradually introduced to more formal academic concepts. The shift is toward building understanding through interactive and discovery-based learning.
    - **Pedagogical Implications:** Pedagogical methods at this stage include visual aids, storytelling with concepts, small group tasks, games that promote logic and thinking, and the introduction of foundational subjects in a child-friendly way. The goal is to encourage conceptual clarity and eliminate rote memorization.
    - **Teaching Method:** Teaching becomes more interactive, using storytelling, illustrations, group activities, and classroom discussions to build conceptual clarity while still maintaining an enjoyable and engaging learning process.
- **Middle Stage (3 years):** Grades 6 to 8 focus on deeper learning in subjects and introduce students to various subjects, encouraging exploration and inquiry.
    - **Pedagogical Implications:** Students are encouraged to ask questions, engage in problem-solving, and participate in projects that combine science, arts, and social issues—reflecting a multidisciplinary approach. Coding, vocational skills, and skill-based modules are also introduced here to promote practical knowledge and future readiness.
    - **Teaching Method:** The teaching approach here includes experiential learning through experiments, projects, and basic research work. Students begin to make connections across subjects and apply knowledge in practical ways, developing analytical and critical thinking skills.

- **Secondary Stage (4 years):** This includes Grades 9 to 12 and allows for greater flexibility in subject choices based on students' interests.
    - **Pedagogical Implications:** The pedagogy here focuses on critical thinking, research, application-based learning, and career orientation. Learners engage in collaborative projects, inquiry-based learning, internships, and presentations. There is a strong shift toward competency-based education, where understanding and skill mastery take precedence over textbook learning. Digital learning tools, self-paced modules, and assessments integrated with learning outcomes support independent thinking and lifelong learning.
    - **Teaching Method:** The teaching methods in this stage encourage independent thinking through case studies, problem-solving tasks, subject integration, and technology-enabled learning. The emphasis is on preparing students for higher education, careers, and life skills.

This structure is not only academic but also developmental, aiming to match the cognitive and emotional needs of learners at each stage. By combining modern teaching methods with traditional Indian educational values (like holistic and personalized learning), NEP 2020 sets a foundation for a more engaging, inclusive, and meaningful education system.

Focus on Holistic and Multidisciplinary Learning

NEP 2020 promotes a holistic approach to education, meaning it aims to develop every aspect of a child—intellectually, socially, emotionally, and physically. Instead of focusing only on academic subjects, schools will encourage students to explore various fields, such as arts, sports, and sciences, fostering creativity and critical thinking.

By integrating multiple disciplines, students can see connections between different subjects, making learning more meaningful and applicable to real-life situations. This approach prepares them to think critically and solve problems creatively, essential skills in today's world.

Importance of Early Childhood Care and Education (ECCE)

Recognizing the vital role of early childhood development, NEP 2020 emphasizes the importance of *Early Childhood Care and Education (ECCE)*. This stage focuses on the development of children from birth to age 6, ensuring they receive the necessary support for their growth.

ECCE programs aim to enhance a child's cognitive, emotional, and physical development through play-based learning. By prioritizing this phase, NEP 2020 lays the foundation for lifelong learning and development, ensuring that children are well-prepared for formal schooling.

Vocational Education and its Integration

NEP 2020 is set to make a big change in how we think about education by introducing vocational education at an early age. This means that students will start learning practical skills alongside their regular school subjects, helping them prepare for future jobs and even encouraging them to become entrepreneurs.

This integration will allow students to learn valuable skills, such as carpentry, plumbing, or computer programming, giving them a head start in their careers. This hands-on experience can also boost their confidence and help them make informed choices about their future paths.

Emphasis on Critical Thinking, Creativity, and Life Skills

In today's fast-paced world, it's essential for students to develop critical thinking, creativity, and life skills. NEP 2020 encourages schools to foster these qualities through innovative teaching methods and experiential learning opportunities.

By prioritizing activities that promote problem-solving, collaboration, and creative expression, the policy helps students become adaptable individuals capable of navigating challenges. This focus prepares them not just for academic success but also for personal and professional growth in the future.

Changes in Assessment Systems (Examinations and Report Cards)

NEP 2020 proposes significant changes in assessment methods to make evaluations more comprehensive and student-friendly. Instead of relying solely on traditional exams, the policy encourages continuous and formative assessments throughout the year.

This means that students will be evaluated on various aspects, such as projects, presentations, and participation in class activities, rather than just final exam scores. Report cards will reflect a more holistic view of a student's performance, highlighting their strengths and areas for improvement. This shift aims to reduce stress and promote a love for learning, rather than a focus solely on grades.

Conclusion

In summary, NEP 2020 is set to transform Indian education by introducing a new structure that focuses on holistic and multidisciplinary learning. By prioritizing early childhood education, vocational skills, and critical thinking, it aims to prepare students for a brighter future. These changes are about more than just academic success; they are about nurturing well-rounded individuals ready to thrive in life. As we embrace these reforms, we move closer to an education system that truly supports every child's growth and potential.

Chapter 4

Transforming Higher Education with NEP 2020

Restructuring Higher Education Institutions (HEIs)

NEP 2020 aims to reshape the landscape of higher education in India by addressing the fragmentation of existing institutions. The policy proposes transforming higher education institutions (HEIs) into large, multidisciplinary universities and colleges. This restructuring will help create **HEI clusters or knowledge hubs,** each accommodating at least 3,000 students, thereby enhancing collaboration and resource sharing among institutions. By 2040, the goal is for all HEIs to evolve into multidisciplinary institutions, allowing for a richer educational experience.

New Framework for Higher Education: Autonomy and Accountability

One of the key features of NEP 2020 is the introduction of a new framework that grants greater autonomy to HEIs while holding them accountable for their performance. This balance of autonomy and accountability aims to encourage institutions to innovate and improve their educational offerings.

With increased freedom in decision-making, universities can design their curricula, set their examination patterns, and introduce new programs based on market demands. At the same time, they will be held responsible for maintaining high standards in education, research, and community engagement. This balance aims to foster innovation and improve the overall quality of higher education.

Transformation in Higher Education Institutions (HEIs)

Before NEP 2020	After NEP 2020
Centrally controlled curricula	Autonomy to design own curricula
Fixed exam and evaluation systems	Freedom to adopt flexible assessment methods
Rigid course structures	Multidisciplinary and modular course designs
Limited accountability for performance	Outcome-based accountability and public disclosures
One-size-fits-all model	Diverse institutional models with unique strengths
Weak industry-academia alignment	Market-relevant programs and stronger linkages

Multidisciplinary Colleges and Universities

NEP 2020 promotes the establishment of multidisciplinary colleges and universities, breaking down traditional barriers between fields of study. This approach encourages students to explore various disciplines, fostering a more comprehensive understanding of complex issues.

The policy aims to provide a broad, multi-disciplinary, and holistic undergraduate education with flexible curricula. It encourages creative combinations of subjects across disciplines and integrates vocational training as an essential part of higher education.

A key innovation in this framework is the introduction of the **"basket system"** for subject selection. Instead of being restricted to rigid streams like science, commerce, or humanities, students can now pick subjects from a wide array of options—just like selecting items from a basket. For example, a student might choose mathematics with music, or history with computer science, or entrepreneurship with environmental studies. This system allows learners to craft a course structure that aligns with both their academic interests and career aspirations, fostering individuality and deeper engagement.

The basket system promotes interdisciplinary learning, encourages exploration beyond traditional boundaries, and helps develop a more well-rounded, adaptable mindset—something especially valuable in a rapidly changing global job market. It reflects the shift from a one-size-fits-all model to a student-centric, choice-based learning environment.

In addition to subject flexibility, the policy offers multiple entry and exit points throughout the undergraduate journey. Students can earn a **certificate after 1 year**, an **advanced diploma after 2 years,** a **Bachelor's degree after 3 years,** and a **Bachelor's degree with Research after 4 years.** This modular structure ensures that every year of study holds value and students can pause and resume their education without losing progress.

An Academic Bank of Credit will be established to digitally store academic credits earned from different higher education institutions (HEIs). This system will enable students to transfer and apply these credits toward their final degree.

Multidisciplinary Education and Research Universities (MERUs)

The National Education Policy (NEP) 2020 emphasizes the establishment of Multidisciplinary Education and Research Universities (MERUs) to promote holistic and flexible learning, comparable to premier institutions like IITs and IIMs. A key aspect of this initiative is enabling students to pursue multidisciplinary education by allowing them to take courses across different branches, colleges, or even universities. Here's how this will work and the role of technology in facilitating it:

1. Flexibility in Multidisciplinary Learning

- **Credit Transfer & Academic Bank of Credits (ABC):**
  - Students can choose subjects from different disciplines (e.g., a Science student studying Economics or an Engineering student learning Design).
  - The **Academic Bank of Credits (ABC)** will digitally store credits earned from various institutions, allowing seamless transfer and accumulation.
- **Multiple Entry-Exit Options:**
  - Learners can pause and resume education, switch institutions, or combine courses from different universities to earn a degree.

2. Role of Technology in Enabling MERUs

Technology will be crucial in implementing this multidisciplinary framework efficiently:

For Students:

- **Online Learning Platforms (SWAYAM, DIKSHA):**
  - Students can access courses from other universities via MOOCs (Massive Open Online Courses).
- **Digital Academic Records:**
  - Blockchain-based credentialing ensures secure and verifiable credit transfers.

- **AI-Powered Guidance Systems:**
  - Recommends interdisciplinary courses based on career aspirations.

For Universities & Administration:

- **Unified University Management System (UMS):**
  - Integrates enrollment, fee payment, and credit tracking across institutions.
- **Automated Credit Recognition:**
  - AI-driven systems validate and map credits from different disciplines.
- **Virtual Labs & Simulation Tools:**
  - Allows students from remote colleges to access high-quality practical training.

For Government & Policymakers:

- **Data Analytics for Policy Decisions:**
  - Tracks enrollment trends, skill gaps, and employability to refine education policies.
- **National Digital Education Architecture (NDEAR):**
  - Provides a standardized tech framework for interoperability between institutions.
- **Fraud Prevention & Transparency:**
  - Blockchain ensures no fake degrees or credential mismanagement.

3. Benefits to the Government

- **Skill Development & Employability:**

    - Produces graduates with diverse skill sets, meeting industry demands.
- **Reduced Infrastructure Burden:**
    - Digital learning reduces pressure on physical campuses.
- **Standardization & Quality Control:**
    - Ensures uniform education standards across MERUs and affiliated colleges.

In short, MERUs are not just about multidisciplinary teaching—they represent a **system-wide shift** toward flexibility, personalization, and smart governance in higher education, driven by technology.

The National Research Foundation will be created as the main organization to promote a strong research culture and enhance research capacity across higher education.

Promoting Research and Innovation

The Indian education system is widely regarded as one of the most credible among developing nations; however, it still has significant room for growth in innovation and entrepreneurship. The National Education Policy (NEP) 2020 aims to reform the current educational framework by emphasizing lifelong learning and fostering an entrepreneurial mindset among students. Moving beyond the traditional pursuit of lucrative job offers, the NEP encourages the younger generation to embrace creativity and critical thinking, essential for driving India's self-reliance and economic growth.

To support this transformation, NEP 2020 promotes the adoption of the **Outcome-Based Education (OBE)** model at all levels of higher education. In this system, academic programs are structured around clearly defined **Program Outcomes (POs)**—broad graduate attributes such as communication skills, ethical reasoning, teamwork, and technical competence. Each subject or course is designed with specific **Course Outcomes (COs)** that contribute directly to these overarching goals. For example, a course in business innovation might have COs like "design a startup model" or "analyze risk in entrepreneurial ventures," which align with POs like "innovation and creativity" or "entrepreneurial competence."

At the college or institutional level, curriculum planners and academic leaders are now required to ensure that their institutional objectives—such as employability, research capacity, or regional development—are mapped to course content through this CO-PO framework. Internal quality assurance cells (IQACs) monitor this alignment to ensure that each subject not only transmits knowledge but also helps students develop industry-relevant skills and attitudes. This structured alignment creates an ecosystem of accountability, where teaching, learning, and assessment are all purpose-driven and measurable.

Through this shift to OBE and structured outcome alignment, NEP 2020 paves the way for an education system that empowers students not just to learn, but to apply, innovate, and lead in real-world settings.

Key initiatives like the National Research Foundation (NRF) and the National Educational Technology Forum (NETF) under the NEP are designed to enhance research and innovation in educational institutions. NRF aims to catalyze quality research through funding and mentorship, while NETF promotes technology-led education from an early age, ensuring students acquire critical skills like coding. By nurturing a culture of innovation and equipping students with the necessary tools, the NEP prepares them not only to excel academically but also to emerge as successful entrepreneurs, ultimately contributing to a self-reliant India.

Internationalization of Higher Education

To establish India as a global study destination, the National Education Policy (NEP) 2020 introduces a range of initiatives aimed at enhancing the internationalization of higher education. This includes facilitating research and teaching partnerships, encouraging Indian universities to set up campuses in other countries, and welcoming top international universities to operate in India. Each higher education institution will also establish an International Student Office to support students from abroad and ensure that credits earned at foreign universities can be recognized.

In line with these goals, the University Grants Commission (UGC) has set guidelines to strengthen internationalization in higher education. As of July 2021, many universities have established Offices for International Affairs and Alumni Connect Cells to better support foreign students. New regulations allow Indian institutions to partner with foreign universities for joint degree programs. Additionally, world-class foreign universities can now operate in Gujarat's GIFT City, aiming to create a high-quality education environment in India. These efforts highlight India's commitment to becoming a leading global education hub.

Conclusion

In conclusion, NEP 2020 is set to transform higher education in India by restructuring institutions, promoting multidisciplinary learning, and encouraging research and innovation. By granting autonomy to universities while ensuring accountability, it aims to create a dynamic educational environment. The focus on internationalization opens doors for students to gain global perspectives. These changes will empower future generations to thrive in a competitive world, making higher education more relevant and impactful than ever before.

Chapter 5

How NEP 2020 Will Impact School Education

Changes in Curriculum and Learning Outcomes

Education is essential for realizing one's potential, building a fair society, and promoting global progress. In India, providing high-quality education for everyone is crucial for economic growth, social equality, scientific advancement, and cultural preservation. With the youth population set to be the largest in the world in the coming decade, India's future depends on offering these young people opportunities for quality education.

The National Education Policy (NEP) 2020 aims to transform the education system from early childhood through higher education. It introduces important changes to the curriculum with a new 5+3+3+4 design. This structure matches learning stages to age groups: the foundational stage (ages 3–8) focuses on Early Childhood Care and Education (ECCE) with hands-on, activity-based learning. The preparatory stage (ages 8–11) continues with playful and discovery-based methods. In the middle stage (ages 11–14), subject teachers will help students explore more complex ideas, while the secondary stage (ages 14–18) will emphasize multidisciplinary study and critical thinking. By making learning more engaging and enjoyable, NEP 2020 seeks to improve education standards and ensure that all students can succeed, regardless of their background.

This new structure aims to move away from memorizing facts and focuses on understanding concepts and applying them in real life. By adding critical thinking, creativity, and life skills to the curriculum, the policy prepares students for future challenges. Learning goals will be clearer, helping students gain important skills and knowledge at every stage of their education.

New Approaches to Student Assessments and Examinations

With NEP 2020, traditional examination methods will be reformed to create a more comprehensive and learner-friendly assessment system. The emphasis will shift from high-stakes, memory-based testing to continuous, formative, and competency-based evaluations conducted throughout the academic year. The goal is to capture not just what students know, but how well they understand, apply, and communicate their knowledge.

The new approach introduces a variety of assessment methods, such as:

- Projects and case studies to encourage research and critical thinking
- Class presentations and group discussions to build communication and collaboration skills
- Peer and self-evaluations to promote reflection and responsibility
- Open-book tests and application-based questions to measure real-world understanding
- Portfolios and experiential learning records to track creative and hands-on skills over time

These methods are designed to assess multiple dimensions of learning—cognitive, emotional, and practical—thereby offering a more holistic picture of a student's progress.

Role of Digital Evolution in Assessments

Technology will play a vital role in this transformation. With the introduction of **AI-powered evaluation tools, digital assessment platforms,** and adaptive testing systems, teachers can track student performance more efficiently and provide personalized feedback. Students will have access to e-portfolios, online quizzes, interactive simulations, and **performance analytics** that support continuous improvement.

For administrators and policymakers, digitized data collection and analytics will help monitor learning outcomes across regions and institutions, enabling better decision-making and targeted interventions.

Ultimately, the NEP envisions an assessment ecosystem that is student-centric, stress-free, and future-ready—one that celebrates progress, encourages curiosity, and supports meaningful learning journeys.

Technology Integration in Classrooms

Incorporating technology into classrooms is a crucial step towards aligning with the National Education Policy (NEP) 2020 across all of India. Integrating technology can transform the teaching and learning process, boost student engagement, and create innovative learning opportunities.

Here are essential steps that schools across India can take to introduce technology effectively in the classroom:

Steps to Introduce Technology in Classrooms for NEP 2020

- **Assess the Infrastructure:** Schools should evaluate their existing infrastructure to identify available technology resources and determine what needs upgrading. This includes hardware like computers, projectors, and tablets, as well as necessary software and online resources.

- **Train Teachers:** Educators must receive training on how to use technology effectively in their classrooms. Professional development programs should be provided to help teachers integrate technology into their teaching methods and ensure they can utilize the available resources.
- **Plan for Equitable Access:** Schools should guarantee that all students have equal access to technology. This can involve providing devices to those who lack technology at home or ensuring students can use tech resources during school hours.
- **Choose Appropriate Technology Tools:** Schools need to select technology tools that align with their teaching goals and curriculum. For instance, video conferencing tools can facilitate online classes and virtual field trips, while learning management systems can help manage course content and assignments.
- **Provide Technical Support:** It's essential to have technical support staff available to resolve any issues with technology resources. This includes keeping hardware and software updated and functioning properly.

Foundational Literacy and Numeracy Mission

The National Policy on Education (NEP, 2020) highlights a critical learning crisis in India, where over 5 crore elementary students lack foundational literacy and numeracy skills, meaning they cannot read basic texts or perform simple arithmetic. This gap in learning leads to persistent underachievement, with many capable students struggling to catch up, which ultimately contributes to school dropout rates. The NEP emphasizes the urgent need to address this issue by establishing foundational literacy and numeracy as a national mission. It calls for comprehensive support from schools, teachers, parents, and communities to ensure that all children have the opportunity for quality education.

To combat this crisis, the Ministry of Education has launched the National Initiative for Proficiency in Reading with Understanding and Numeracy (NIPUN Bharat), aiming for every child to achieve foundational literacy and numeracy by the end of Grade 3 by 2026-27. This initiative includes clear learning outcomes for children from preschool to Grade 3 and emphasizes competency-based education and continuous assessment. Moreover, the program seeks to engage parents and communities to foster a collaborative environment for learning. By leveraging digital platforms like DIKSHA for teacher training and community involvement, the FLN Mission strives to empower all stakeholders in this crucial educational endeavor.

Conclusion

As we explore how NEP 2020 impacts school education, it's clear that these changes aim to create a more effective, engaging, and inclusive learning environment. These changes are designed to create a brighter future for students, helping them grow into confident and capable individuals ready to take on the world.

Chapter 6

Challenges in Implementing NEP 2020

Bridging the Urban-Rural Divide

One of the key challenges in implementing NEP 2020 is addressing the stark differences between urban and rural education systems. While urban schools may have access to better resources, facilities, and technology, many rural schools face a lack of infrastructure and trained teachers. Ensuring equal opportunities for all students, regardless of where they live, will require significant effort in building infrastructure, improving digital access, and providing better support for rural educators.

Teacher Training and Development

Teachers play a central role in bringing the vision of NEP 2020 to life. However, many teachers across India are not yet trained in the new teaching methods, technology integration, or the updated curriculum that NEP 2020 requires.

The National Education Policy (NEP) emphasizes empowering teachers through continuous professional development and capacity-building initiatives, ensuring they are well-prepared from the grassroots level. The policy focuses on key areas like teacher recruitment, with a minimum qualification of a four-year integrated

B.Ed., and ongoing classroom support. NEP introduces Continuous Professional Development (CPD), requiring teachers to undergo at least 50 hours of training annually, along with mentorship from experienced professionals.

Additionally, the NEP promotes the NISHTHA program, a holistic training initiative aimed at improving the skills of teachers and school heads across elementary and secondary levels. This structured approach ensures teachers are equipped with the necessary skills to foster high-quality education.

Infrastructure and Resource Constraints

The success of NEP 2020 heavily depends on the availability of adequate infrastructure and resources, including classrooms, digital tools, and learning materials. Many schools, particularly in rural areas, are lacking in basic facilities like clean drinking water, proper sanitation, and electricity, let alone access to advanced technology. Addressing these resource gaps is critical to ensure that the policy can be implemented effectively across all regions.

Resistance to Change: Cultural and Societal Challenges

Introducing a new education system also means overcoming resistance to change from various sections of society. Cultural traditions, long-standing beliefs, and societal expectations can sometimes stand in the way of implementing new ideas and approaches. Parents, teachers, and local communities may need time and awareness campaigns to understand and embrace the benefits of NEP 2020. Shifting these mindsets will be a gradual process, requiring patience and consistent efforts.

Financial Implications for Implementation

The implementation of the National Education Policy (NEP) 2020 brings significant financial implications, especially concerning India's commitment to increase public spending on education from 4.4% to 6% of GDP. This proposed increase aims to address long-standing discrepancies between the targeted and actual investments in education. The policy emphasizes the need for substantial investments in infrastructure, technology, and teacher training to support the reforms, including a flexible curriculum, early childhood education, and multidisciplinary courses in higher education.

However, achieving these goals will require overcoming key financial challenges. For example, enhancing teacher and student resources, improving infrastructure, and providing access to technology and inclusive education for all will necessitate increased financial allocation. Additionally, expanding multidisciplinary programs in higher education will require further investments in new facilities and faculty. If successfully implemented, NEP 2020 could play a crucial role in aligning India's education system with global standards, but its success heavily depends on the timely mobilization of financial resources.

Conclusion

In summary, NEP 2020 brings many positive changes, but there are challenges to overcome. Bridging the gap between cities and villages, training teachers well, and improving school resources will take time and effort. We also need to change traditional thinking and find enough funds to support these plans. With determination and teamwork, these challenges can be tackled to create a better future for all students.

Chapter 7

The Best Strategies to Implement NEP 2020

Role of Government, Private Sector, and NGOs

Role of Government

The government plays a pivotal role in the implementation of NEP 2020. Its responsibilities include:

- **Policy Framework:** Establishing a clear policy framework that outlines the objectives and strategies of NEP 2020, ensuring alignment with national educational goals.
- **Resource Allocation:** Allocating adequate financial resources to support initiatives under NEP 2020, such as infrastructure development, teacher training, and technology integration.
- **Regulation and Oversight:** Setting up regulatory mechanisms to monitor the quality of education across institutions and ensure compliance with the new standards established by the policy.
- **Capacity Building:** Facilitating training programs for teachers and administrators to equip them with the skills needed to implement the new curriculum and teaching methodologies effectively.
- **Public Awareness:** Promoting awareness about NEP 2020 among stakeholders, including educators, parents, and students, to foster a supportive environment for its implementation.

Examples of State-Level Government Initiatives

Several states in India have already taken proactive steps to implement NEP 2020. Examples include:

- **Karnataka:** Became the first state to formally implement NEP 2020 in higher education. The state introduced four-year undergraduate degree programs with multiple exit and entry points and adopted digital platforms like LMS (Learning Management Systems) for blended learning.
- **Uttar Pradesh:** Launched the "School Chalein Hum" initiative to promote foundational literacy and numeracy aligned with NEP goals. It also initiated teacher training programs to ensure classroom readiness for the new curriculum.
- **Madhya Pradesh:** Rolled out NEP-aligned modules in state-run colleges, including competency-based assessments, digital classrooms, and extensive faculty orientation drives.
- **Delhi:** Focused on early childhood care and education (ECCE) with the introduction of play-based learning and curriculum revisions in government preschools under the NEP framework.
- **Tamil Nadu & Kerala:** Although initially cautious, these states have initiated curriculum reforms and consultation workshops to align parts of their existing education systems with NEP's broader goals, especially in teacher education and digital learning.

These state-level actions demonstrate the **crucial enabling role of the government** not only as a policymaker but also as an active facilitator and collaborator in NEP 2020's rollout.

Role of Private Sector

The private sector is essential for complementing government efforts in education. Its contributions include:

- **Investment in Education:** Providing financial resources for building infrastructure, developing educational technologies, and creating innovative learning solutions that align with NEP 2020 goals.

- **Quality Education Delivery:** Offering high-quality educational services and programs that can serve as models for public institutions, especially in areas where government schools may lack resources.
- **Collaboration with Public Institutions:** Engaging in public-private partnerships (PPPs) to share best practices, resources, and expertise. This collaboration can enhance educational outcomes and expand access to quality education.
- **Innovation in Teaching Methods:** Introducing new teaching methodologies and curricula that focus on skill development, critical thinking, and creativity, thereby enriching the overall educational landscape.
- **Supporting Vocational Training:** Developing vocational education programs that provide students with practical skills relevant to the job market, thus addressing the skills gap highlighted in NEP 2020.

Role of NGOs

Non-governmental organizations (NGOs) play a crucial role in supporting the implementation of NEP 2020 by:

- **Advocacy and Awareness:** Raising awareness about educational issues and advocating for marginalized communities to ensure their voices are heard in policy discussions.
- **Community Engagement:** Mobilizing communities to participate actively in educational initiatives, fostering a sense of ownership and accountability among local stakeholders.

- **Capacity Building:** Providing training and resources for teachers and school administrators in underserved areas to improve the quality of education delivered.
- **Monitoring and Evaluation:** Assisting in monitoring the progress of NEP 2020 implementation at the grassroots level, providing feedback to policymakers on challenges faced by schools and communities.
- **Innovative Programs:** Developing and implementing innovative educational programs that address specific local needs, such as literacy campaigns or skill development workshops.

Strengthening Teacher Training Programs

One of the most effective ways to bring about lasting change is through strong teacher training. Well-trained teachers are the driving force behind educational reform. New training programs need to go beyond basic skills and focus on equipping teachers to handle modern teaching methods, new curricula, and digital tools. This way, they can inspire students to embrace holistic learning, creativity, and critical thinking. It's also important to provide ongoing support, so teachers can keep learning and improving throughout their careers. When teachers feel confident and well-prepared, they can make a big difference in their students' education and help them succeed.

Public-Private Partnerships in Education

Public-private partnerships (PPPs) can play an important role in implementing NEP 2020. These partnerships can help with sharing resources, building better facilities, and introducing new teaching methods. For instance, private institutions can work together with government schools to provide teacher training or create special programs for students. Such collaborations combine the strengths of both public and private sectors to improve educational outcomes.

This way, schools can access more tools and expertise, making education better for everyone. By joining forces, we can create more opportunities for students and ensure they receive a quality education.

Effective Monitoring and Evaluation Systems

Without proper monitoring, even the best plans can fail. Having an effective evaluation system is crucial to ensure that the goals of NEP 2020 are being met. Schools, teachers, and administrators can track their progress, fix problems, and celebrate their successes. By using data and feedback, they can see what's working and what isn't, which helps shape future policies. Regular check-ins allow everyone to stay on track and make necessary adjustments. This commitment to monitoring and evaluation is key to making sure that the vision of NEP 2020 becomes a reality in every classroom.

Role of Parents and Communities in Implementation

Parents and communities are essential in making NEP 2020 a reality. They support children outside the classroom, reinforcing what's taught in school. By being involved in their children's education, attending meetings, and giving feedback, parents and local communities ensure the reforms are relevant and effective. Their participation helps create a stronger connection between home and school. When parents collaborate with teachers, it benefits the students' learning experience. Additionally, when communities come together to support education, it creates a positive environment that encourages students to thrive and succeed in their studies.

Conclusion

In summary, putting NEP 2020 into action needs teamwork from many people, including the government, private companies, NGOs, teachers, parents, and communities. By improving teacher training, working together with private organizations, setting up good monitoring systems, and involving parents and local communities, we can build an education system that meets the needs of all students and helps them prepare for the future.

Chapter 8

The Role of Technology in NEP 2020

The National Education Policy (NEP) 2020 is a visionary blueprint for India's education system. At its core, it aims to create a holistic, learner-centric, and technology-enabled education ecosystem. Imagine a classroom where learning knows no boundaries, where students from remote villages connect seamlessly with educators across the globe. This is not just a dream; it is the reality we can achieve through the innovative use of technology in education.

Leveraging Digital Learning Platforms

Digital learning platforms are revolutionizing education by making high-quality resources accessible to every learner. Whether it's interactive videos, online courses, or virtual classrooms, technology breaks down the barriers of geography and socio-economic status. Students can engage with diverse content at their own pace, fostering a personalized learning experience that enhances understanding and retention. The NEP 2020 emphasizes this shift, urging educational institutions to adopt digital solutions that empower learners to take charge of their education.

E-Learning and Remote Education: Opportunities and Challenges

The rise of e-learning and remote education opens a world of opportunities, particularly in a country as vast and diverse as

India. Imagine a student in a remote village accessing the same educational resources as a student in a metropolitan city! However, this shift comes with its challenges. We must confront issues like digital literacy, access to devices, and internet connectivity. NEP 2020 acknowledges these barriers and outlines strategies to build a robust digital learning ecosystem that ensures equitable access to quality education for all.

1. Government LMS Platforms and Tools

Several government initiatives have introduced Learning Management Systems (LMS) and digital repositories to support schools, teachers, and learners:

- **DIKSHA (Digital Infrastructure for Knowledge Sharing):** A government-backed platform that offers digital textbooks, teaching videos, practice exercises, and assessment tools for students and teachers across grades.
    - Teachers can upload or create content, track student learning, and access training modules.
    - Content can be added using the DIKSHA mobile app or web portal after creating an account with verified teacher credentials.
- **SWAYAM:** A national platform offering MOOCs (Massive Open Online Courses) for higher education students, available in multiple Indian languages. It also integrates courses from top institutions like IITs and IGNOU.
- **ePathshala:** A joint initiative of NCERT and the Ministry of Education, offering eBooks, audio-visual materials, and teacher training resources.
- **PM eVidya:** Combines TV channels, radio, and online content under a unified digital education campaign, reaching students in remote areas with no internet access.

2. Creating and Uploading Video Content

To enhance learning through multimedia, teachers and content creators can:

- **Record lectures using free tools like:**
  - **OBS Studio (Open Broadcaster Software):** Ideal for screen recording and live streaming.
  - **Screencast-O-Matic or Loom:** Easy-to-use screen recorders with webcam integration.
- **Edit videos using:**
  - OpenShot or Shotcut (free video editing tools)
  - Add captions, visuals, and effects to make lessons more engaging.
- **Upload content to:**
  - DIKSHA (after account approval by school/authority)
  - YouTube (private or public channels for class-wise content)
  - Google Drive or OneDrive for sharing within school networks

3. Best Free Methods to Create E-Content

Educators can use free, user-friendly tools to create and share interactive lessons:

Tool	Use Case	Link
Canva	Create visually appealing slides and infographics	canva.com
Google Forms	Create quizzes, polls, or feedback	forms.google.com

Padlet	Collaborative whiteboard or discussion space	padlet.com
Quizizz / Kahoot!	Game-based assessments and revision	quizizz.com, kahoot.com
Nearpod	Create interactive presentations with real-time response	nearpod.com

By promoting low-cost digital content creation, expanding government LMS usage, and improving connectivity infrastructure, NEP 2020 sets the stage for a more inclusive, tech-enabled learning environment. With the right training and tools, even small schools in rural areas can become hubs of interactive and personalized digital education.

Use of AI, AR/VR, and Data Analytics in Education

The integration of cutting-edge technologies like Artificial Intelligence (AI), Augmented Reality (AR), Virtual Reality (VR), and data analytics is set to transform the educational experience. AI can personalize learning by adapting to each student's unique needs, while AR and VR create immersive environments that bring lessons to life, making complex concepts tangible. Imagine studying the solar system not just from a textbook but by exploring it in a virtual space! Data analytics provides invaluable insights into student performance, helping educators tailor their teaching strategies. The NEP 2020 encourages the adoption of these technologies to create a dynamic and engaging learning ecosystem.

Role of Technology in Bridging Gaps: Inclusive Education for All

Technology plays a key role in closing educational gaps and making learning accessible for everyone. It offers tools for children with disabilities, providing different ways to connect with lessons. With assistive technologies and online resources, all students can join in the learning process. These tools can include speech-to-text software and learning apps that cater to various needs. The NEP 2020 supports this idea of inclusive education, aiming to create a space where everyone is valued and can reach their full potential. By making education more accessible, we help all students face challenges and succeed.

Digital Infrastructure Development: Building a Future-Ready Education System

For technology to make a real difference in education, strong digital infrastructure is essential. This means not just having reliable internet but also creating safe online platforms for learning and teamwork. A good digital setup makes it easier for students to access valuable information and resources. The NEP 2020 encourages significant investments in digital infrastructure, ensuring that schools are ready to keep up with new technology trends. By building a future-ready education system, we can give our students the skills they need to succeed in a fast-changing world. This focus on digital growth will help prepare learners for future challenges.

Streamlining Campus Operations: Effective Management through ERP Systems in Education

In today's data-driven academic environment, managing large educational institutions demands a high level of coordination and efficiency. To meet this need, **Enterprise Resource Planning (ERP)** systems are becoming vital tools in streamlining campus operations across India. Aligned with the goals of NEP 2020, ERP systems help institutions adopt a more organized, transparent, and tech-enabled management structure.

ERP software integrates all key administrative and academic functions of a school, college, or university into a single digital platform—from admissions, fee management, and examination processing to library services, HR, inventory, and alumni engagement.

Key Benefits of ERP Systems in Education

- **Centralized Data Management:** All student and staff data—from enrollment to attendance and exam results—is stored in one unified system, ensuring easy access and improved decision-making.
- **Automation of Routine Tasks:** Administrative tasks like generating ID cards, issuing certificates, calculating grades, and scheduling classes are automated, reducing manual errors and saving time.
- **Improved Transparency and Accountability:** Real-time tracking of student progress, staff activities, and institutional finances enhances accountability at every level.
- **Parent and Student Portals:** ERP systems often include web and mobile apps that allow students and parents to check attendance, grades, fees, assignments, and announcements from anywhere.
- **Regulatory Compliance:** ERP systems generate reports required by accreditation bodies (like NAAC, NBA, UGC) efficiently, helping institutions maintain compliance without added workload.
- **Resource Optimization:** From managing classrooms and laboratories to allocating faculty and scheduling exams, ERP software helps institutions make the best use of their physical and human resources.

Alignment with NEP 2020 Vision

NEP 2020 envisions a digitally empowered education system that operates with efficiency, transparency, and responsiveness. ERP systems support this vision by:

- Facilitating data-driven governance at all levels—from classroom to campus to ministry.
- Enabling real-time monitoring and evaluation of policy implementation.
- Supporting multi-campus collaborations, such as shared digital libraries, faculty exchange programs, and joint certification efforts.

Incorporating ERP systems is no longer optional for forward-looking institutions—it is essential for scaling quality, ensuring compliance, and preparing for a multi-disciplinary, flexible, and tech-integrated future envisioned by NEP 2020.

Conclusion

In conclusion, the role of technology in NEP 2020 is not just about integrating new tools into the classroom; it is about reimagining the entire educational experience. It's about empowering learners, creating inclusive environments, and preparing future generations for the challenges ahead. As we embrace this technological revolution, let us stand up, take action, and shape a brighter future for education in India. The time for change is now—let's harness the power of technology to transform lives!

Chapter 9

Global Education Systems vs. Indian Education System

When we think about education, it's fascinating to see how different countries approach teaching and learning. Each system has its unique strengths and challenges. In this chapter, we'll take a closer look at some key global education systems, compare them with the Indian education system, and see what lessons we can learn for the implementation of the National Education Policy (NEP) 2020.

Overview of Key Global Education Systems

Let's start with a quick tour around the world! Countries like **Finland** and **Singapore** are often highlighted for their impressive education systems. Finland focuses on creativity and critical thinking rather than standardized tests, allowing students to learn in a relaxed environment. They emphasize equal opportunities for all students, regardless of their background.

On the other hand, Singapore is known for its rigorous curriculum and strong emphasis on math and science. Their students often excel in international assessments, thanks to a well-structured system that prepares them for real-world challenges. Both countries have unique methods that make learning engaging and effective.

Comparison of Indian and Global Models

Now, how does our Indian education system stack up against these global examples? When we compare the Indian education system with global models like Finland and Singapore, we can spot several key differences. Here are four important factors to consider:

1. **Assessment Approaches:** One major difference is how students are assessed. In Finland and Singapore, the focus is on holistic development and practical skills. Students are encouraged to think critically and apply what they learn in real-life situations. In contrast, the Indian education system often relies heavily on exams, which can lead students to memorize information instead of truly understanding it. This exam-centric approach can create stress and pressure, making learning less enjoyable.
2. **Teacher Training:** Teacher training is another important factor. In Finland, teaching is a respected profession, and teachers receive extensive training to help them innovate in the classroom. They are empowered to design their own lessons and adapt to their students' needs. In India, while we have made progress in teacher training, many educators still lack sufficient resources and ongoing support to feel fully equipped and inspired to teach effectively.
3. **Curriculum Design:** The design of the curriculum also differs. In countries like Singapore, the curriculum is focused on depth rather than breadth. Students dive deep into a few subjects, which helps them gain a better understanding. In contrast, the Indian curriculum can be quite rigid and content-heavy, requiring students to cover a lot of material without fully grasping it. This can lead to a lack of interest in learning. The NEP 2020 aims to make our curriculum more flexible and engaging, and we can learn from global practices to achieve this.

4. **Student Engagement and Well-Being:** Finally, student engagement and well-being are crucial. Finnish schools prioritize the emotional and social well-being of their students, allowing time for breaks and play. This approach fosters a love for learning and reduces stress. In India, there is often a stronger emphasis on academic performance, which can lead to anxiety among students. The NEP 2020 acknowledges the need for better mental health support and aims to create a more balanced educational experience for our students.

Lessons from Global Education Practices for NEP 2020 Implementation

So, what can we learn from these global practices for our own NEP 2020? First, we need to shift our focus from just grades to overall student development. This means encouraging creativity, problem-solving, and critical thinking skills in our classrooms.

We can also take inspiration from Finland's emphasis on play and enjoyment in learning. By making education fun and engaging, we can help students develop a love for learning that lasts a lifetime. Additionally, investing in teacher training and support is crucial to creating a positive learning environment.

How NEP 2020 Aligns with Global Educational Trends

The good news is that NEP 2020 aligns closely with many global educational trends, placing India on a progressive path toward building a 21st-century learning ecosystem. The policy's emphasis on holistic development, skill-based learning, and flexible curriculum design mirrors key frameworks adopted by countries leading in educational innovation.

Key Global Trends Reflected in NEP 2020

Global Trend	NEP 2020 Alignment
Holistic Education	Emphasis on physical education, arts, ethics, emotional well-being, and life skills across school stages.
21st Century Skills	Focus on communication, collaboration, creativity, and critical thinking (the 4Cs).
Flexible Learning Pathways	Multiple entry-exit options in higher education, multidisciplinary undergraduate degrees.
Vocational Integration	Vocational education from Grade 6 onward; aim to involve 50% learners in vocational programs by 2025.
Technology Integration	National Educational Technology Forum (NETF), digital infrastructure (DIKSHA, SWAYAM), ERP systems.
Foundational Literacy and Numeracy (FLN)	Goal to achieve universal FLN by Grade 3 by 2026-27 (aligned with SDG Target 4.1).
Research and Innovation	Creation of MERUs and NRF to encourage original research and global academic collaboration.

The Statistical Backbone of NEP 2020:

1. Gross Enrollment Ratio (GER):

India's GER in higher education was around 27–28% in 2019–20. NEP 2020 aims to reach 50% by 2035, a significant leap driven by multidisciplinary degrees and online options.

Ref: [https://www.reddit.com/r/india/comments/1f6cn07]

Ref:[https://prsindia.org/policy/report-summaries/national-education-policy-2020]

2. Vocational Education Expansion:

Less than 5% of youth (age 19–24) had vocational exposure before NEP. With its rollout, 50% exposure by 2025 is now the target—aligned with countries like Germany and South Korea.

Ref: [https://nep2020.hinsoli.com/2020/08/nep-2020-part-ii-higher-education_74.html]

3. Digital Learning Growth:

During the COVID-19 period, online learning usage surged by over 300% in India. The DIKSHA platform registered approximately 5.8 billion sessions with 292,000 pieces of live content by mid-2022.

Ref: [https://www.linkedin.com/pulse/evolution-indias-education-system-what-nep-2020-means-rajput-unevc]

4. SWAYAM Platform Reach:

SWAYAM, India's national MOOC portal, has recorded 1.21 crore unique users and over 4 crore enrollments, reflecting strong uptake in open digital learning

Ref: [https://en.wikipedia.org/wiki/SWAYAM]

Moreover, NEP 2020 promotes the use of technology in education, allowing students to access a wealth of knowledge beyond textbooks.

This is similar to how many global systems are integrating digital tools to enhance learning experiences.

Key Areas of Alignment and Innovation

1. Effective Operation through ERP and Campus Management Solutions

NEP 2020 promotes the modernization of educational institutions by encouraging the use of **Enterprise Resource Planning (ERP)** systems. These digital platforms streamline operations such as:

- Student admissions and academic records
- Fee management and finance
- Hostel and library systems
- Real-time attendance and performance tracking
- Internal communication and document automation

These systems not only reduce manual work and paper usage but also enable institutions to function efficiently and transparently—mirroring global trends in **smart campus management.**

2. NAAC, NBA, and Other Accreditation Mechanisms

In line with international quality standards, NEP 2020 supports outcome-based education (OBE) and regular assessments through bodies like:

- NAAC (National Assessment and Accreditation Council)
- NBA (National Board of Accreditation)
- NIRF (National Institutional Ranking Framework)

These frameworks align with international benchmarking systems such as QS Rankings and Times Higher Education, ensuring that Indian institutions maintain high academic standards, transparency, and accountability. Accreditations now also evaluate the Course

Outcomes (CO), Program Outcomes (PO), and their alignment with institutional objectives.

3. Introduction of Robotics and Future Technologies

Recognizing global interest in **robotics, AI, and automation**, NEP 2020 recommends introducing **coding and robotics** as early as Grade 6. This prepares students for future careers in technology, in line with international initiatives like:

- STEM curriculum reforms in the US and UK
- Robotics Labs in South Korea and Japan
- AI education pilots in Europe and Australia

Robotics labs, hands-on learning kits, and AI-enabled virtual tutors are being introduced to help Indian students build 21st-century skills early on.

4. Auto-Secure Question Paper Delivery Systems

NEP 2020 also acknowledges the need to improve the examination process. To prevent question paper leaks and ensure integrity, many universities are adopting automated, encrypted question paper delivery systems. These systems allow:

- Time-bound unlocking of encrypted files
- Decentralized access control
- Tamper-proof transmission from central servers to examination centers

This is a major step toward digitizing examination systems, aligning with secure practices adopted by global testing agencies like ETS (TOEFL, GRE) and Cambridge Assessment.

Together, these innovations help Indian education evolve into a globally competent and future-ready system.

Conclusion

In summary, as we explore global education systems and compare them with our Indian model, it becomes clear that there's much we can learn. By embracing the lessons from countries like Finland and Singapore, we can enrich our education system, making it more effective and inclusive for every student. NEP 2020 is a step in the right direction, and with the right mindset, we can create a bright future for education in India. Let's take inspiration from around the world and work together to shape an education system that prepares our children for the challenges and opportunities ahead!

Chapter 10

Outcome-Based Education (OBE) and Its Role in NEP 2020

What is Outcome-Based Education?

Outcome-Based Education (OBE) is an educational approach that centers learning around the final outcomes — what learners are expected to know and be able to do after completing a course or program. It shifts the focus from traditional teaching methods and input-based metrics (like syllabus coverage and class hours) to measurable student achievements and competencies.

In simpler terms, OBE asks:

- What should a student be able to do after learning this?
- How will we measure whether the student has achieved that outcome?

Instead of focusing on completing a curriculum, OBE ensures that the curriculum, teaching methods, and assessments are all designed to achieve specific learning outcomes.

Key Components of OBE

1. Program Outcomes (POs)

Program Outcomes are broad competencies students are expected to achieve by the time they graduate from a particular program (e.g., B.Tech, B.Com, BA). These include skills like critical thinking, problem-solving, communication, lifelong learning, and ethical responsibility.

Example of a PO for an engineering program:

- "Graduates will be able to apply mathematical, scientific, and engineering principles to solve real-world problems."

2. **Course Outcomes (COs)**

Course Outcomes are specific to individual courses or subjects. Each CO should align with one or more POs. These outcomes describe what a student will be able to do after completing a course.

Example of a CO for a math course:

- "Students will be able to apply linear algebra techniques to solve engineering problems."

CO-PO Mapping

This mapping helps ensure that every course in a program contributes meaningfully toward achieving the broader Program Outcomes.

➢ A CO-PO Matrix is used to show the strength of relationships between each CO and the POs. These relationships are typically rated as:

- 1 = Low
- 2 = Medium
- 3 = High

This matrix helps identify which courses are strongly contributing to certain outcomes, and which need revision.

Teaching and Learning Methods in OBE

- **Active Learning:** Includes group discussions, peer teaching, and case studies to promote engagement.
- **Project-Based Learning:** Encourages application of concepts to real-life scenarios.
- **Blended Learning:** Combines online resources with traditional classroom methods.
- **Collaborative Learning:** Builds communication and teamwork skills.

These methods are chosen based on the nature of the outcomes expected from students.

Assessment and Evaluation in OBE

Assessment in OBE is continuous and multidimensional. It includes:

- **Direct Assessments:** Tests, assignments, presentations, lab work, projects.
- **Indirect Assessments:** Surveys, feedback from students, alumni, and employers.

Each assessment item is tagged to specific COs. The attainment of outcomes is calculated as a percentage and helps institutions know how well students are achieving the desired skills.

Example:

If 75% of students score above a certain threshold in a CO-aligned question, it is considered “Attained.”

NEP 2020 and Integration of OBE

The National Education Policy (NEP) 2020 advocates for flexibility, multidisciplinary learning, and skill development — all of which align with the philosophy of OBE. NEP encourages institutions to:

- Design learning outcomes for all programs.
- Offer flexible course structures with exit and entry points.
- Focus on application-based, experiential, and competency-driven education.

With OBE, NEP ensures students are job-ready, socially responsible, and adaptable to changing global demands.

Benefits of Implementing OBE

- Clarity: Students and teachers know the exact goals.
- **Transparency:** Easy tracking of learning and teaching effectiveness.
- **Improved Quality:** Continuous improvement based on feedback and assessment.
- **Global Acceptance:** Aligns with international education standards, enhancing global mobility for students.

Conclusion

Outcome-Based Education is not just a system — it's a philosophy that puts learners and learning outcomes at the center. Through clear objectives (POs and COs), strategic mapping, and meaningful assessments, OBE ensures that Indian students receive an education that is relevant, skill-oriented, and aligned with the vision of NEP 2020. As more institutions adopt OBE, India moves closer to a learner-centric and globally competent education system.

Chapter 11

The Future of Education in India: A New Dawn

As we look ahead, the future of education in India is bright and full of promise. With the National Education Policy (NEP) guiding us, we can expect significant changes in the coming decade. Let's explore how Indian education will evolve, prepare students for a global economy, align with Sustainable Development Goals (SDGs), and foster a culture of lifelong learning.

How Indian Education Will Change Over the Next Decade with NEP

By 2030, Indian education will create a lively and welcoming environment for students. Imagine classrooms buzzing with energy, where children actively participate in fun activities and discussions. Instead of just memorizing facts, they'll be working on real-world problems that help them think critically and creatively.

Schools will feel more like community centers, connecting students with local businesses and mentors who can guide them in their learning journey. With technology integrated into the classroom, even students in remote areas will have access to resources and learning tools that enhance their education. Picture using virtual reality to explore historical events or scientific concepts firsthand, making learning come alive!

Teachers will be key players in this new setup. They won't just stand in front of the class lecturing; instead, they'll encourage students to express themselves and discover their strengths. The focus will also be on the emotional and social well-being of students, ensuring everyone feels valued and supported.

In this bright future, Indian education will not just prepare students for jobs but will help them grow as individuals. It's an exciting time ahead, where every child will have the chance to shine and make a difference!

Preparing Students for a Global Knowledge Economy

In today's world, knowledge is key to success. The NEP aims to equip Indian students with the skills and knowledge they need to thrive in a global economy. By emphasizing practical skills and hands-on experience, we will prepare our youth for various careers, including those in technology, healthcare, and entrepreneurship. This preparation will help them compete not just locally but also globally, giving them the confidence to shine on any stage.

Aligning Indian Education with Sustainable Development Goals (SDGs)

Aligning Indian education with the United Nations Sustainable Development Goals (SDGs) is a critical endeavor that aims to address pressing socio-economic and environmental challenges. The SDGs, comprising 17 goals and 169 targets, were adopted by all 193 UN member states to eradicate poverty, enhance education, reduce inequality, and promote sustainable economic growth by 2030. India's National Education Policy (NEP) 2020 plays a pivotal role in this alignment, particularly focusing on quality education and inclusivity.

NEP 2020 and Its Alignment with SDGs

- **Quality Education (SDG 4):** NEP 2020 emphasizes foundational literacy, holistic development, and competency-based learning, aligning with SDG 4's goal of inclusive and quality education. By prioritizing essential skills and innovative teaching methods, NEP 2020 helps achieve SDG 4 targets like improving learning outcomes and enhancing educational access.
- **Gender Equality (SDG 5):** NEP 2020 recognizes gender equality in education and proposes measures to eliminate gender disparities. By promoting equitable access and empowering girls, it supports SDG 5 targets, ensuring equal educational opportunities and reducing gender-based discrimination.
- **Reduced Inequalities (SDG 10):** NEP 2020 focuses on equity and inclusion, aiming to eliminate disparities based on socio-economic status and geography. By providing quality education for marginalized groups, it contributes to SDG 10 targets, reducing inequalities within and among countries.
- **Quality of Life and Well-being (SDG 3):** Education plays a vital role in promoting health and well-being. NEP 2020's emphasis on holistic development and mental health support aligns with SDG 3's aim for healthy lives. By fostering students' overall well-being, it aids in achieving SDG 3 targets like reducing maternal and child mortality.
- **Partnerships for the Goals (SDG 17):** Achieving the SDGs requires collaboration among various stakeholders. NEP 2020 stresses stakeholder engagement and community participation in education reform. By fostering partnerships, it contributes to SDG 17 targets, strengthening global collaborations for sustainable development.

- **Employability and Skills Development (SDG8):** NEP 2020 focuses on equipping students with practical skills that enhance employability. This includes integrating vocational training into the curriculum and fostering a culture of entrepreneurship among students, thereby contributing to SDG8 (Decent Work and Economic Growth).

Building a New Culture of Lifelong Learning

Learning is no longer confined to the four walls of a classroom or limited to one stage of life. The National Education Policy (NEP) 2020 envisions an **education system that nurtures continuous learning, growth, and self-improvement** across an individual's lifetime. Here's how NEP 2020 lays the foundation for this powerful shift:

1. Promoting Practical and Hands-On Learning

NEP 2020 moves away from rote memorization and embraces experiential learning. This includes:

- Project-based learning, simulations, and real-life problem-solving integrated into school and college curricula.
- Workshops, labs, and field visits that allow students to connect theory with application.
- Encouraging students to participate in community-based projects and innovation challenges to solve real-world issues.

By doing rather than just reading, students learn how to apply knowledge in meaningful ways—skills that stay with them for life.

2. Fostering an Entrepreneurial Mindset

NEP 2020 doesn't just aim to create job-seekers—it wants to cultivate job-creators. To do this:

- Schools and colleges are encouraged to offer entrepreneurship as part of their curriculum.
- Entrepreneurship cells and startup clubs will be promoted within institutions to expose students to business planning, innovation, and leadership.
- Students will learn how to identify problems, design solutions, and pitch ideas, supported by mentors and industry leaders.

This mindset develops **risk-taking, creativity, and self-confidence,** preparing students to shape their own future ventures.

3. Making Students Industry-Ready

To bridge the gap between academia and the job market, NEP 2020 focuses on producing career-ready graduates by:

- Integrating vocational education from as early as Grade 6, allowing students to gain practical skills alongside academics.
- Encouraging internships and apprenticeships through partnerships with industries and local businesses.
- Promoting skill-based certifications that align with current and emerging industry needs.

The goal is to ensure that students not only have degrees but also the competence and confidence to enter the workforce directly.

4. Supporting Startups and Innovation at the Student Level

NEP 2020 recognizes the potential of young innovators and aims to provide the ecosystem they need:

- Institutions will be encouraged to set up incubation centers and innovation hubs on campus.
- Students will have access to resources, mentorship, and funding opportunities to turn ideas into startups.
- Courses on design thinking, business modeling, and digital entrepreneurship will become more common.

This approach supports grassroots innovation and fosters the next generation of changemakers.

5. Creating a Lifelong Learning Ecosystem

NEP 2020 promotes a vision where learning doesn't end with a degree. Instead, it becomes a continuous process by:

- Encouraging online learning platforms and modular courses that people can access at any age.
- Establishing credit banks so learners can accumulate and transfer credits across institutions and return to education whenever they wish.
- Supporting reskilling and upskilling programs for professionals in response to evolving technologies and job markets.

This ensures that every citizen, whether a student, professional, or retiree, has the freedom and flexibility to grow.

NEP 2020 doesn't just reshape schooling; it inspires a national mindset shift toward **lifelong, practical, and purposeful learning.** By embracing hands-on education, entrepreneurial thinking, and career readiness, India is preparing its youth not just for the jobs of today—but to lead the innovations of tomorrow.

Conclusion

In conclusion, the future of education in India is set for a remarkable transformation with NEP 2020 leading the way. By focusing on flexible learning, global preparedness, sustainable development, and lifelong education, we are paving the path for our youth to succeed in an ever-changing world. Together, we can nurture a generation of learners who are not only equipped with knowledge but also passionate about making a difference in their communities and the world. This new dawn in education will empower our students to shine brightly and achieve their dreams!

Chapter 12

Conclusion: Empowering Future Generations Through Education Reform

India is on the verge of a major change in education, thanks to the National Education Policy (NEP) 2020. This policy aims to improve the way we learn and teach, making education more fair and competitive on a global level. As we look at how NEP 2020 will impact our future, it's clear that education reform is essential for empowering the next generation.

The Impact of NEP 2020 on India's Global Competitiveness

NEP 2020 has a bold vision for India to become a global leader in education, similar to its historical role as a center of knowledge with famous institutions like Nalanda University. One of the key goals is to increase the number of students enrolled in higher education from 26.3% in 2018 to 50% by 2035. This means more people will have access to quality education.

The policy also focuses on teaching practical skills and offers vocational training, ensuring that over 50% of students will receive some form of vocational education by 2025. This is important because it prepares students for real-world jobs.

Additionally, NEP encourages partnerships with foreign universities. Indian universities can set up campuses abroad, and top international institutions can establish branches in India. This exchange of knowledge not only improves the quality of education but also makes India an attractive destination for international students, aiming to boost enrollment from 50,000 to 200,000 by 2030.

Long-Term Vision for Education in India

The long-term goal of NEP 2020 is to create an education system that encourages critical thinking, creativity, and innovation. By integrating technology into learning and promoting research through initiatives like the National Research Foundation, the policy aims to equip students with skills needed for today's job market.

A significant part of this vision is making education flexible. Students will have multiple options for entering and exiting their studies, allowing them to learn at their own pace and choose subjects that interest them. This flexibility is crucial as it prepares students for a rapidly changing world.

A Call to Action: Collaborating for Transformative Education

For NEP 2020 to succeed, everyone must work together—government officials, schools, businesses, and communities. By joining forces, we can create an environment where innovation and excellence thrive in education.

Schools are encouraged to adopt successful practices from around the world while still honoring Indian culture and values. For example, including subjects like Yoga and Indian history can attract international students interested in learning about India's rich heritage. Additionally, forming partnerships with businesses will help ensure that educational programs meet current job market needs.

In conclusion, NEP 2020 marks an exciting step toward transforming India's educational system. By focusing on fairness, quality, and global competitiveness, it empowers future generations with the knowledge and skills they need to succeed in a connected world. As we embrace this new chapter in education reform, let's work together to make this vision a reality—turning India into not just a center of knowledge but also a source of inspiration for learners around the globe.

I hope the information provided in this book has been beneficial for you and that you have gained sufficient and important insights about NEP 2020.

If you still have any questions or if there's anything else you'd like to understand about any topic or want to give any feedback or input, you can directly schedule a one-on-one meeting with me using the email address provided below.

Email ID: bhavesh@infinityinfoway.com

Warm Regards,

Bhavesh Kumar Gadhethariya

The road ahead is filled with opportunities; let's take this chance to build a brighter future through transformative education!